This book was written on October 12, 2009 and completed from top to bottom within those 24 hours. It was a test of my endurance, creativity and spiritual awaking.

There are 24 poems. One for each hour of the day.

OTHER BOOKS BY ROBERT M. DRAKE

Spaceship (2012)

Science (2013)

Beautiful Chaos (2014)

Black Butterfly (2015)

A Brilliant Madness (2015)

Beautiful and Damned (2016)

Broken Flowers (2016)

Seed Of Chaos (2017)

Gravity: A Novel (2017)

Moon Theory (2017)

Young & Rebellious (2018)

Chasing The Gloom (2018)

Samuel White & The Frog King (2018)

For Excerpts and Updates please follow:

Instagram.com/rmdrk
Facebook.com/rmdrk
Twitter.com/rmdrk

ISBN: 978-0-9986293-7-7

Book Cover: Robert M. Drake
Cover Image licensed by Shutter Stock Inc.

For Sevyn, For Summer

All my words are yours.
All of my words, will always be yours.

CONTENTS

THE CITY AND YOU	1
BLOOMING TONIGHT	3
THE CLOUDS AND YOU	4
A PLACE	6
SPACESHIPS	11
SO LOW, TOO LOW	13
PEOPLE LEAVE	15
YOUR TIME TO LET GO	17
WHAT YOU NEED	19
WHERE WE COME AND WHY	21
SPECIAL IN YOUR EYES	23
THE DOOM IS DAY	25
YOUR SHELL IS NOT A HOME	27
LOVE HER	31
REMEMBER REMEMBER	33
IT IS LATE...	36
THIS THING NOW	38
PRESSING THE GRAIN	41
HARD TO FEEL, TO KNOW	45
THE GODS	50
KEEP TO YOURSELF	54
GONE GONE GONE	57
THE TYPO	63
LIKE YOU...	66

THE GREAT ARTIST

& THE 24 HOUR PROJECT

ROBERT M. DRAKE

THE CITY AND YOU

You were always fascinated
with the city.

The loud sounds
and the way cars would pass.

And I never understood why.

I mean,
you had it all... right?

Where you stood,
friends, family,

good music and good food.

And now that you are gone…

I understand why you wanted
to get away so much,

why you wanted
to leave.

You had your own dreams,

some...

none of us were meant
to understand but you.

I'm glad you are chasing them

and I am glad

you are brave enough

to do
what you have to do.

Let the Gods bless you
in your journey.

Let the Gods guide you
when you need it.

And let the Gods
be there for you...

when you feel the need
to fall apart.

BLOOMING TONIGHT

You have to bloom
the best way you know how.

You have to realize
that the sun is *your* sun

and that the soil
is *your* soil

and you have to grow
the way you were meant

to grow.

Do not try
and become someone else.

Do not think

and feel how you are told to.

If you do not agree with something...
then it is okay.

Not many people will understand this...
because not many people

know who they are.

THE CLOUDS AND YOU

Look at the clouds.
Look at the sky.

Look at the world around you.

Do you not see beautiful things?

Do you not see
all the movement going on,

even during the latest times
at night?

Everything around you is surviving,
fighting for a chance to live.

So there is no reason for you
to want to end it all.

No reason for you
to want to run away
and start over.

Life begins right here
and to be reminded of that,

all you have to do is
open your eyes,

pay close attention
and let it all consume you.

There are answers everywhere
to your questions

and they can change your life
but only

if you allow them to.

A PLACE

There is a place
in our hearts
that don't belong to us.

That'll never belong
to us.

No matter how hard
we try to retrieve it back.

No matter how hard
we try to break in.

And we lose this part
of ourselves

with the first person
we fall in love with.

The first moment
you look into their eyes.

This space.
This star.

This universe
inside your heart.

Spinning,
dizzy and full of love.

You can feel it
but you can't see it—

you don't have access to it
when you need to shut it off.

When you need it
to settle down.

This place.
This island.

This dungeon of love.

It keeps me up at night.

The soft music
keeps playing

over and over again.

This place,
I tell you

will be the end of me,
of all of us.

This little dark space

of hope.

Full of hidden laughter.

Full of joy.
Full of life.

It's contagious,
this I tell you,

it's spreading to the other parts
of my heart.

Then down the veins
then toward the brain.

Then from the brain
to the body.

And I can feel it.
All of it.

This little space crowded,
looking for a way out.

Looking for a way
to defeat me.

And I know it is there.

I know it wants to be heard—felt.

I know all these things
about this place,

although, I have never been there.
I'm not allowed.

This place.
It gives me superpowers.

It gives me breath
when I feel like I am drowning.

And it makes my days
a little easier to get through—

a little brighter
to see straightforward.

This space…

ring the alarms.

Let the dogs out
and secure the area.

This place is on tonight
and it is beginning to draw a crowd

and it is all because of you.

It is all

because you exist
and because you

are always here…
in this place.

You are in my heart
when no one is around

and I love you
I always have.

Many moons before
you called this place

your home.

SPACESHIPS

It felt
like a spaceship
coming from the stars.

Like the earth
being hit by a comet.

Like landing
on another planet

and being surrounded
by nothing you know.

It was uncomfortable.

It was hard,
uneasy and restless...
but I wanted it.

I wanted you.
All of you.

And to be honest,
I was scared at first

but now I am not afraid
of opening up to you.

Now I am not afraid of opening
up to anyone, really.

Some will say I have matured.
Some will say I have learned
my lesson.

And some will say it was
due to timing.

I say it was all because of you.

I'm a different person now
and I want to thank you

for all that you have done.

You have made me realize
so much

and you have made me feel
out of this world.

SO LOW, TOO LOW

It is okay
to feel low sometimes.

It is okay
not to know

or understand what it is
you are feeling.

We have all
gone through these moments.

We have all
been through hell
and back.

Depression is no walk in the park,
and I mean *real* depression.

The kind you feel
when everything is going right

but all you can do
is sit down and cry.

It's okay to break apart.
It's okay to not know why.

It's okay to cry and cry and cry.
To contradict yourself and not
know who you are sometimes.

Just remember,
that when you do…

I will be here for you.
I will always be here

when you need
me the most.

I will be your shoulder
to lean on

and I will bring you back
from the grave

whenever you feel

like you can't breathe.

PEOPLE LEAVE

People leave.

They leave traces behind.

They leave their memories
lingering, haunting those

who once loved them.

It hurts,
that I know,

that *we all know*

and loving someone
always puts you
in a vulnerable position.

Prone to getting hurt.
To getting your heart broken.

And still, *knowing* this...
we all commit to someone

sometimes...

we all ignore
the outcomes.

We make up
to break up

and there isn't a reason
in the world

that could explain

why.

YOUR TIME TO LET GO

This is your time
and I know

you know it is.

Your time
to move on.

Your time to heal.
Your time to learn

something new about yourself.

To learn
how the world ticks—works
and how it doesn't.

This is your time, kiddo.

Believe it.
Believe in yourself

but *really* believe
as if your life depends on it.

As if the lives
of the people you love
depends on it.

This is your time
to do all the things

you've always wanted to do.
To let go of the regret—

to get help if needed
and to set your demons free.

This is *your* time, my friend.

It always is.
A positive change
is always beyond your grasp.

All you have to do
is reach a little harder,

make the effort
and believe

that all good things
do indeed

come to those
who really want it

and *really try.*

WHAT YOU NEED

Sometimes
you need your own
space to heal.

Because yes,
although,

it is fair and beautiful
to have people

who understand
what you are going through

it is also necessary
to figure things out

on your own.

Because that is how it happens.

You are born alone.
You grow alone.
You heal and shatter…

alone.

And yes,
some will stand by you.

Some will even
ease the pain away...

but you have to face
these things alone

and only you

have the courage
to overcome

whatever it is
that hurts.

WHERE WE COME AND WHY

We come from different places.

We come from different backgrounds.

I see you
and you see me.

This is how
we blend together
and become one.

This is how
we set our differences aside.

This is how
we end discrimination,

racism
and the other things
that divide us.

This is how...

by opening our hearts
and seeing people

for who they are.

For whom they can be.

I know it is a bit
naive of me

but hey, it is a start.

And there is nothing wrong
with having a little hope.

With having a dream.

Amen.

SPECIAL IN YOUR EYES

There is something special
in your eyes.

The way they speak to me.
The way they express
what I feel.

You know me
and without exchanging

any words.

You understand me
when I'm confused.

You're always by me
when I'm sad.

And you never leave my side
no matter what.

If only there was something
I can do

to show you
how much I care.

To show you

how much I need you.

This I say,

to all the dog owners
around the world.

Love your dog,
hug them

and do not ignore them.

They need you
more than you need them.

They need your love

more

than anything else.

THE DOOM IS DAY

There are too many things
that bring us closer
to our doom.

Too many
lost moments

gone missing
in a blink of an eye.

Too many
people looking for other people
to love.

Too many
feelings going unnoticed

and too many
hearts longing to be held.

And this is my art.
This is how I bleed.

How I express
what I hold within.

These are my words...
full of contradictions,

confusion and empty roads.

This is what I go through
when you are not around.

This is how I survive.

In all places
that are lonely

and all places that exist
but have no meaning

because *you*

are not here.

Rest easy, my brother.

YOUR SHELL IS NOT A HOME

You want to hide
within your shell

because you do not want people
to get too close

or make judgements of you.

So you stay behind the scenes.
Behind the walls of solitude—

behind your eyes
and face.

Deep within your chest
where your loneliness dwells.

You stay inside there
and you do not make

a sound

because you do not want
anyone to notice you.

You do not want
anyone to care,

anyone

to show you
how you are capable
of more.

And this is how you live your life.

Afraid of love.
Afraid of rejection
and acceptance.

Afraid of people
not taking you seriously.

You're afraid of all these things
that can mean so much to you.

I *can't believe*
you're living this way.

I can't believe
you believe

that you don't deserve more.

And I can't believe
your doubts are getting the best of you.

It's hard,
I know,

breaking free.

Taking off
and not looking back.

It's hard
but you cannot hide
in your shell forever.

You cannot overlook
the people who genuinely

want to get to know you.

You're going to drown
within yourself, you know?

Cave in
and possibly never come out

because

one day,
you are going to have to come out
for some fresh air.

One day,
you are going to have to

face your fears
and let people love you

for who you are.

Let people
get to know you.

And it doesn't have to be *now*
but one day, you know…

one day,
you're going to be okay
with all of this...

and believe me
your becoming will be beautiful.

That I promise you.

Just take your time,
keep your heart open

and come out of your shell
when it's the right time
to do so.

After that,
everything will fall into place.

Everything will mean
so much more.

LOVE HER

She wants you to love her.

Is that too much to do?
Is that too much to commit?

She wants you
to give her *your* time.

To give her *your* attention.

She does not want flowers.

She does not want cards
or even the world.

She only wants *your* time
and she wants you to appreciate hers.

She wants late night conversations,
morning texts and random kisses.

She wants the little things.

She wants you
to comfort her

when she feels most alone
and she wants someone

to talk to…

when she is on the edge
of it all.

Someone to pull her away
from her doom.

That is all she needs.
That is all she wants.

Pay attention to her.

Is that not
why you wanted her
in the first place?

Is that not
why you wanted her love?

Love her.
Care for her.

And do not let
one day pass

without making her feel
how lucky you are

to have her in your life.
That is all.

REMEMBER REMEMBER

Do you remember
the good times?

When we were young
and in love?

Do you remember
those late nights we stayed up

together

till sunrise
holding each other
because everything around us
hurt?

Do you remember
when I first met you?

And how shy you were
to mention my name?

Do you remember
the last time I told you

how much I loved you?

How much I appreciated you

for all the things you do?

Do you rememeber
what your life was
before me?

Because I surely don't
and frankly,
I don't even care.

Because since the moment I met you,
it has been you.

And I know
since the moment you met me,

you felt
what I felt

and that's beautiful.

It really *is* something special,
something to hold on to proudly.

And now the world
is in chaos

and all we have
is each other,

so we should love

and spread love more
than before.

And remind the people
we care about most...

how to love.

IT IS LATE...

It is late,
and I am sure

you have someone
to go home to.

Someone
to share a meal with,

a conversation with.

I am sure
you have someone

who listens to your troubles
and worries.

And how blessed are you
to have at least

one person

to be there for you.

One person who understands.
One person who really cares

with all heart and soul.

This is your bestfriend.
This is your soulmate.

Your lover.
Your teacher, healer.

Take this with you
no matter how far you go.

No matter how many
people you meet.

Through the corners of the earth...

you are blessed.

You are so blessed
and you barely even know it.

Take a moment,
look around you...

you have the whole
goddamn universe smiling at you

and those who love you
and you love—

the most.

THIS THING NOW

I have this thing now
and I don't know

what it is
or what to call it.

But since
my daughter has been born.

I feel more alive.

More appreciative
of what I do.

What I eat.
What I think and feel

and how I approach
certain things.

I told my cousin, Hex
about this and he said,

 *"You're just maturing now,
growing now."*

But I don't think it's that.
I think it's something else.

I think it's

me

living for someone else.

Me

making sure I'm alive
and well for someone else.

You've ever had that feeling?

That feeling that you're
no longer in control.

You're no longer
driving the wheel.

That's how *it* feels.

Like I'm living
just to make sure I'm there
to watch her grow.

This must be
what it's like

to be in love—real love.

The kind that'll make you

change your entire life.

The kind
that has you reaching for more.

The kind
you could only find
in a child.

This must be
what it feels like.

Anything else
wouldn't make much sense

at all.

PRESSING THE GRAIN

I know what it feels like
to have something resting
on your chest.

Something pressing down
on it—making it difficult
for you to breathe.

I know what it's like
to have your heart jitter.

So fast
that you'd think

any moment now
you're bound to greet death,

your maker.

I know what it's like
to owe something to someone

without having
what you need
to pay them back.

I know what it's like
to have your heart broken

and still
go to work the next day
as if nothing is happening.

I know,
and I think we all *know*.

But here's what I've learned
about people.

And here's what I've learned
to differentiate… friends from foe.

Know the difference.

A friend will genuinely care
and it is something you'll feel

without the exchange of words.

They'll sit with you
comfort you

even if you keep repeating yourself
over and over.

A foe will take your breaking point
for their own amusement.

They don't
want to see you rise,

they get a thrill
while watching you fall.

And they'll keep milking you
for what hurts,

only to spread rumors
and lies about you

without you
even noticing it.

This is something
you, too, will feel.

Beware with what your heart
is telling you

no matter how broken it is,
it still has the power to feel.

And trust it.

Sometimes it knows more
than the mind.

More than what your thoughts
are telling you.

Follow it.
Trust it

and your true friends.

Slay the demons
and keep your eyes open for snakes...

they're everywhere.

HARD TO FEEL, TO KNOW

It's hard to feel.

I remember who I was
before I met you.

I remember
what it felt like
to be myself.

What it felt like
to be free.

To be happy.

Now I know,
this always starts bad.

Hell,
but life isn't perfect
and neither is love.

And I *loved* her.
I really did.

I gave her the best parts of me...
and the worst.

But someway,

somehow,
I still managed to mess things up.

I still managed
to let her drown

before my eyes.

Now I put this on
my grandmother's bones.

I swear,
I *did* try.

I did give it all I had.

*(I am not just writing it,
to have something to write about.)*

I did
and it drove me mad.

It drove me
out of my element.

Full of rage.
Full of hatred—jealousy.

I loved her
but I also hated her.
Loved her for what she made me feel

when we were okay.

And hated her
for the way she would

fuck with my heart
whenever she wanted to.

It was hard, you know?

Getting in control
cause once you're in...

you're all in.

Fuck!

And I'm a lot tougher than that.
A lot stronger, too.

But damn she had me.
She had me the moment I met her.

The moment she smiled.

And she got the best of me.

I should have known,
she was fucked up even more

than I was

but nonetheless,

she really put a number on me.

She sent me to hell
with words

and

I've never been the same since.

I've just been here,
breathing, barely alive...

surviving, you know?

It's hard for me to be real here.

It's hard for me
to write things like this.

Just know
that right now

in this very moment,
I am vulnerable

and my typewriter
is playing devil's advocate.

It's telling me to bleed,

to keep going, to keep writing—drinking...

for the sake
of my own good.

While knowing
deep down inside

it is ultimately,
the road to my very doom.

THE GODS

You belong amongst the gods.

Amongst the flowers.
Amongst the clouds.

This I say
to you

with all of my love
and respect:

but I could tell you're tired
of the bullshit.

I could tell
you're sick of it,

and I can
because you're living your life

as if your waiting for it
to pass you by.

As if you're counting
all the seconds ticking on the clock,

bored

because you feel like nothing
is connecting for you.

Like nothing is making any sense.

And I could tell
something is bothering you

and it's probably something
you've been holding in

for a *very long time.*

Maybe even something
you're ashamed of speaking about,

embarrassed,
afraid of.

Maybe you don't have
anyone you can trust.

Or maybe you've raked
enough snakes;

too many

to even think
you have people to talk to.

I say this to you

with all my love,
with all my respect:

I want to be here for you.
I want to help you.

And I know I'm coming off
as being intense

and maybe even a little intimidating.

But there's something in your eyes
that's piercing through my soul.

Calling out to me, you know?

And maybe you don't see it
or feel it

but I do.

Loud and clear.

You're searching for something
or someone

and maybe that person is me.

I just hope you
give me a chance
because for you...

I'm willing to lose everything.

Im willing to give it all up
for a shot at love.

For a shot to show
and prove to you

that you are capable of happiness.

And that

you're capable
of letting all

the bullshit go.

KEEP TO YOURSELF

You can keep to yourself.

You can keep
as quiet as you'd like.

You can run far
and never return home.

One day
someone is going to
get a hold of you.

And I don't mean
physically grab you

and keep you still.

I mean emotionally.
I mean spiritually.

And they will break you down.

They will captivate you
and you will feel things.

Some, perhaps,
you've never felt before.

Now I know this is a lot
to take in

and some will even be afraid
of it, avoid it, too,

at all cost.

But as I write to you...

I am letting you know
that this will happen.

That there is no getting around this.
It's mandatory.

Getting hurt *is* mandatory.
Falling in love *is* mandatory.

And all the aches that come with it,

all mandatory.

So there are no short cuts
to finding happiness.

These are the paths
we must go through.

So you can keep to yourself
all you want

but one day,
you'll lose your heart.

You'll watch it slowly
slip away

and make it's way
into someone else's palm.

So please,
decide responsibly.

Please give it to someone
worth it.

You deserve to love someone naturally
in an unnatural way.

Stay wild.
Stay free.

And above all,
stay beautiful,

my friends.

GONE GONE GONE

And one day
she will be gone.

One day
she will walk out of your life

and she will not think
twice about it.

And the good times
will disappear.

And the laughter
will find a halt.

And the texts
will stop coming in.

And the calls and voice messages
will suddenly vanish.

And you will notice
and reality will hit you

like a car
speeding on the freeway.

And you will wonder

what has become of her.

You will wonder
when

and why did it end
so abruptly.

And it will be like
waking up from a dream.

And you will wish
you were still dreaming.

And your world will slowly
start piling down.

And you will feel
like you're falling.

Like you're not able
to get yourself back together.

And everything you know
will become a fantasy.

And the only thing
that will be real

is the fact
that *you lost her*.

And it will sting like nothing else.

It will hurt like no other.
And the pain will paralyze your body.

Your mind.
Your heart.

And your soul.

And the only thing
you'll be able to look back upon

is the last night
you saw her.

And her face will haunt you.

It will be in all places,
especially in those

where you feel most alone.

And you will try to reach her
but it will be *too late*.

Because it'll always be
too late.

And you will regret it
for the rest of your life.

And you will learn
how to cope with it—with the lack

of attention you gave her.

And you will learn from it.

And you will try not to commit
this again.

And the next one you love,
will be easier to love.

And the next one
will make you smile,

will bring out your laughter
as she once did.

And the next one
will help you ease the pain

and you will believe
that you're okay

but you won't be

because none of them
will be her.

They will all

remind you of her
and they will always take you back

to those golden days
when you had her.

She will become
the one you let slip away.

Now all of this might sound troubling
but all of this could

also be avoided.

Love her.
Cherish her.

Help her when she's down.

Help her when she
needs it most.

Pay attention to her.
Get to know her.

What she loves
and what she doesn't love.

Become her friend
but also her lover.

Listen to her.
Acknowledge her flaws

and never lose sight
of why you wanted her

in the first place.

She is yours
and you are hers.

And you should never think otherwise.

This is love
and you should treat love

with kindness
and respect.

Always.

THE TYPO

Please forgive me
for the typo.

The thing is,
I'm an artist.

I don't have time
for the academic conformities.

I don't have time
to follow the rules,

to bend them,
to break them.

It's hard for me
to abide by them.

To live by them.

I write from the soul
and the soul doesn't worry

about these standards.

It doesn't worry
if you call this poetry or prose.

Good or bad writing.

It doesn't matter
because it is my own

and it represents what *I feel.*
What I've been through.

My dreams,
my ambitions,

my horrors and all.

This is my work
and ironically,

these are my rules.

I am free. I am free. I am free.

The margins do not represent me.
They do not control what I do.

How I do it and why.

But still,
my sweet people,

please forgive me
for the typo
for I know it can ruin

a good poem,
a good book

but please don't be
so hard on something you enjoy.

Don't place it toward the road
of perfection

because

nothing is
and nothing has to be.

So please,
before you turn the page.

Enjoy what you love
and enjoy it well...

savor it
and don't take it *too* serious.

The moment you do
it loses its meaning.

It loses its purpose
and loses...

its soul.

LIKE YOU...

Like you...

I, too, filter my pain
through laughter,

through good company
and good liquor.

And like you, I, too,
have many questions.

Some about life.
Some about the people

who've left me
and some about why I feel

the way I feel—am
the way that I am...

about how different
things would be

if I gave a lot of things
a chance

and if I gave
the people I've lost

a little more.

Because we're the same.

Our hearts are lost searching
for the right places to rest in.

They are lost looking
for the right people to call home.

And like you,

I ask myself almost every night...
how long does it take

to save someone's soul?

How long does it take
to get over someone?

How long does it take
to forget the things

that bring us pain.

And how long does it take
to go.

So I could see
why you want to let go.

I could see
why you want to end things,
move on, you know?

I could see

the emptiness
becoming more empty

and the darkness swallowing
the light.

I could see all of these things
through your eyes.

Through the way you softly speak.

This is your truth
and it is mine, too.

We are lovers
that want to love

but we give ourselves
to the wrong kind of people.

And hell,
you might think it's your fault
but I think it's not.

I think it's in your DNA

to love, to give, to accept
even when you know

it is wrong.

How long does it take
to move on? You ask?

Sometimes, a lifetime.

How long does it take
to save someone's soul?

Sometimes, forever.

And how long does it take
to get over someone?

Sometimes, never.

So all these things that trouble you,
trouble, me, too.

They keep me up at night.

They bring both chaos
and horror to my heart.

I'm sorry to have to end this
this way... confused
and loss for words.

But before you close this book.

I just want you to know
that you're not alone

and how sometimes,
it's not very easy to say

good-bye.

I know I'm a little
all over the place

with this one.

I just want to write
the way I feel

and I want to express myself
the best way

I know how.

CPSIA information can be obtained
at www.ICGtesting.com
Printed in the USA
FSHW02n0828050918
52040FS

9 780998 629377